The Long Road Turns To Joy

The Long Road Turns To Joy

A Guide to Walking Meditation

Thich Nhat Hanh

Parallax Press
Berkeley, California

An earlier version of this book, *A Guide to Walking Meditation*, was published by
Fellowship Publications, Nyack, New York, in 1985 and is now out of print.
Cover photo by Simon Chaput. Thich Nhat Hanh leading walking meditation at the
reflecting pool in front of the Lincoln Memorial, Washington, D.C., November 1990.
Back cover photo by Simon Chaput.
Calligraphy on page 1 by Thich Nhat Hanh.
Drawing on page 81 by Vo-Dinh Mai.
Cover and book design by Legacy Media, Inc.

Library of Congress Cataloging-in-Publication Data
Nhât Hạnh, Thích.
    [Thiên hành yéu chi. English]
    The long road turns to joy : a guide to walking meditation / Thich
Nhat Hanh.
      p. cm.
    Rev. ed. of: A guide to walking meditation. 1985.   ISBN 0-938077-83-X (pbk.)
    1. Meditation—Buddhism.   2. Buddhist meditations.   I. Nhât Hạnh, Thích.
Guide to walking meditation.   II. Title.
BQ5618.V5N5313 1996
294.3'443—dc20
                                                                              96-19559
                                                                                  CIP

5   6   7   8   9   10   /   05   04   03   02   01

Contents

I have arrived
I am home
in the here
in the now
I am solid
I am free
in the ultimate
I dwell

Anyone Can Do It

Walking meditation is meditation while walking. We walk slowly, in a relaxed way, keeping a light smile on our lips. When we practice this way, we feel deeply at ease, and our steps are those of the most secure person on Earth. All our sorrows and anxieties drop away, and peace and joy fill our hearts. Anyone can do it. It takes only a little time, a little mindfulness, and the wish to be happy.

The Present Moment

The Buddha was asked, "What do you and your disciples practice?" and he replied, "We sit, we walk, and we eat." The questioner continued, "But sir, everyone sits, walks, and eats." The Buddha told him, "When we sit, we know we are sitting. When we walk, we know we are walking. When we eat, we know we are eating."

Most of the time, we are lost in the past or carried away by the future. When we are mindful, deeply in touch with the present moment, our understanding of what is going on deepens, and we begin to be filled with acceptance, joy, peace, and love.

Everything Depends on Your Steps

The seed of mindfulness is in each of us, but we usually forget to water it. We think that happiness is only possible in the future—when we get a house, a car, a Ph.D. We struggle in our mind and body, and we don't touch the peace and joy that are available right now—the blue sky, the green leaves, the eyes of our beloved.

What is most important? Many people have passed exams and bought houses and cars, yet they are still unhappy. What is most important is to find peace and to share it with others. To have peace, you can begin by walking peacefully. Everything depends on your steps.

Aimlessness

In Buddhism, there is a word, *apranihita*. It means wishlessness or aimlessness. The idea is that we do not put anything ahead of ourselves and run after it. When we practice walking meditation, we walk in this spirit. We just enjoy the walking, with no particular aim or destination. Our walking is not a means to an end. We walk for the sake of walking.

A. J. Muste said, "There is no way to peace, peace *is* the way." Walking in mindfulness brings us peace and joy, and makes our life real. Why rush? Our final destination will only be the graveyard. Why not walk in the direction of life, enjoying peace in each moment with every step? There is no need to struggle. Enjoy each step. We have already arrived.

Touching Peace

If you think that peace and happiness are somewhere else and you run after them, you will never arrive. It is only when you realize that peace and happiness are available here in the present moment that you will be able to relax.

In daily life, there is so much to do and so little time. You may feel pressured to run all the time. Just stop! Touch the ground of the present moment deeply, and you will touch real peace and joy.

Walk in Peace

If you look deeply, you can see all the worries and anxiety people print on the Earth as they walk. Our steps are usually heavy, filled with sorrow and fear. We feel insecure, and our steps reveal it.

This world has many paths. Some are lined with beautiful trees, some wind around fragrant fields, some are covered with leaves and blossoms. But if we walk on them with a heavy heart, we will not appreciate them at all.

When we were one or two, we began to take tottering steps. Now, we have to learn to walk again—slowly, with joy and ease. After a few days of practice, you will know how to do it. When I see you walking with deep comfort and peace, I will smile happily.

Smile like a Buddha

As you make the effort to let go of your worries and anxieties, please smile. It may be just the beginning of a smile, but keep it there on your lips. It is very much like the Buddha's half-smile. As you learn to walk as the Buddha walked, you can smile as he smiled. Why wait until you are completely transformed, completely awakened? You can start being a part-time Buddha right now!

The half-smile is the fruit of your awareness that you are here, alive, walking. At the same time, it nurtures more peace and joy within you. Smiling as you practice walking meditation will keep your steps calm and peaceful, and give you a deep sense of ease. A smile refreshes your whole being and strengthens your practice. Don't be afraid to smile.

Regaining Our Sovereignty

Your smile proves that you are not a colony, that you have sovereignty over yourself, that you are doing your best. The Buddha is sometimes called, "One who has Sovereignty over Himself or Herself." Events carry us away, and we lose ourselves. Walking meditation helps us regain our sovereignty, our liberty as a human being. We walk with grace and dignity, like an emperor, like a lion. Each step is life.

Touching the Earth

When he was challenged by Mara—who personifies delusion—the Buddha touched the Earth with his right hand and said, "With Earth as my witness, I will sit here in meditation until I realize true awakening." When he did that, Mara disappeared.

Sometimes we too are visited by Mara—when we feel irritated, insecure, angry, or unhappy. When that happens, please touch the Earth deeply with your feet. Please practice walking meditation. The Earth, our mother, is filled with deep love for us. When we suffer, she will protect us, nourishing us with her beautiful trees, grasses, and flowers.

Healing Mother Earth

Walking mindfully on the Earth can restore our peace and harmony, and it can restore the Earth's peace and harmony as well. We are children of the Earth. We rely on her for our happiness, and she relies on us also. Whether the Earth is beautiful, fresh, and green, or arid and parched depends on our way of walking. When we practice walking meditation beautifully, we massage the Earth with our feet and plant seeds of joy and happiness with each step. Our Mother will heal us, and we will heal her.

Conscious Breathing

The core practice taught by the Buddha was mindfulness, including mindfulness of breathing: "Breathing in, I know I am breathing in. Breathing out, I know I am breathing out." It is like drinking a glass of cool water. As we breathe in, we really feel the air filling our lungs. In sitting meditation and in walking meditation we practice like this, paying close attention to each breath and each step.

Counting

While walking, practice conscious breathing by counting steps. Notice each breath and the number of steps you take as you breathe in and as you breathe out.

If you take three steps during an in-breath, say, silently, "One, two, three,"or "In, in, in," one word with each step. As you breathe out, if you take three steps, say, "Out, out, out," with each step. If you take three steps as you breathe in and four steps as you breathe out, you say, "In, in, in. Out, out, out, out," or "One, two, three. One, two, three, four."

Breathe Naturally

Don't try to control your breathing. Allow your lungs as much time and air as they need, and simply notice how many steps you take as your lungs fill up and how many you take as they empty, mindful of both your breath and your steps. The link is the counting.

When you walk uphill or downhill, the number of steps per breath will change. Always follow the needs of your lungs. Do not try to control your breathing or your walking. Just observe them deeply.

A Marvelous Balance of Mindfulness

When you begin to practice, your exhalation may be longer than your inhalation. You might find that you take three steps during your in-breath and four steps on your out-breath (3-4), or two steps/three steps (2-3). If this is comfortable for you, please enjoy practicing this way. After you have been doing walking meditation for some time, your in-breath and out-breath will probably become equal: 3-3, or 2-2, or 4-4.

Don't forget to practice smiling. Your half-smile will bring calm and delight to your steps and your breath, and help sustain your attention. After practicing for half an hour or an hour, you will find that your breath, your steps, your counting, and your half-smile all blend together in a marvelous balance of mindfulness.

Stay with Your Breathing

If you see something along the way that you want to touch with your mindfulness—the blue sky, the hills, a tree, or a bird—just stop, but while you do, continue breathing mindfully. You can keep the object of your contemplation alive by means of mindful breathing. If you don't breathe consciously, sooner or later your thinking will settle back in, and the bird or the tree will disappear. Always stay with your breathing.

Getting More Fresh Air

After you have been practicing for a few days, try adding one more step to your exhalation. For example, if your normal breathing is 2-2, without walking any faster, lengthen your exhalation and practice 2-3 for four or five times. Then go back to 2-2.

In normal breathing, we never expel all the air from our lungs. There is always some left. By adding another step to your exhalation, you will push out more of this stale air. Don't overdo it. Four or five times are enough. More can make you tired. After breathing this way four or five times, let your breath return to normal. Then, five or ten minutes later, you can repeat the process. Remember to add a step to the exhalation, not the inhalation.

Improved Circulation

After practicing for a few more days, your lungs might say to you, "If we could do 3-3 instead of 2-3, that would be wonderful." If the message is clear, try it, but even then, only do it four or five times. Then go back to 2-2. In five or ten minutes, begin 2-3, and then do 3-3 again.

After several months, your lungs will be healthier and your blood will circulate better. Your way of breathing will have been transformed.

Interbeing

In Plum Village, the community of practice where I live in France, everyone always walks in walking-meditation style. Every time we go from one place to another, even a short distance—to the meditation hall, the dining hall, or even to the toilet—we walk mindfully like that.

Whenever I see someone walking mindfully, she or he is a bell of mindfulness for me. Seeing her walk mindfully, I touch the peace, joy, and deep presence of her being, and the peace, joy, and deep presence of myself.

Using Words Instead of Numbers

We can practice walking meditation by counting steps or by using words. If the rhythm of our breathing is 3-3, for example, we can say, silently, "Lotus flower blooms. Lotus flower blooms," or "The green planet. The green planet," as we walk. If our breathing rhythm is 2-3, we might say, "Lotus flower. Lotus flower blooms." Or "Walking on the green planet. Walking on the green planet," for 5-5. Or "Walking on the green planet, I'm walking on the green planet," for 5-6.

We don't just say the words. We really see flowers blooming under our feet. We really become one with our green planet. Feel free to use your own creativity and wisdom. Walking meditation is for your enjoyment. It is not hard labor.

I Have Arrived

You can also practice walking meditation using the lines of a poem. In Zen Buddhism, poetry and practice always go together.

> I have arrived.
> I am home
> in the here,
> in the now.
> I am solid.
> I am free.
> In the ultimate
> I dwell.

Our True Home

When we practice walking meditation, we arrive in each moment. Our true home is in the present moment. When we enter the present moment deeply, our regrets and sorrows disappear, and we discover life with all its wonders. Breathing in, we say to ourselves, "I have arrived." Breathing out, we say, "I am home." When we do this, we overcome dispersion and dwell peacefully in the present moment, which is the only moment for us to be alive.

Here and Now

It is enjoyable to practice with the words of a verse like "I Have Arrived." As you breathe in, you say "Arrived" with each step, and as you breathe out, you say "Home" with each step. If your rhythm is 2-3, you will say, "Arrived, arrived. Home, home, home," coordinating the words and your steps according to the rhythm of your breathing.

After practicing "Arrived/Home" for awhile, if you feel relaxed and fully present with each step and each breath, you can switch to "Here/Now." The words are different, but the practice is the same.

Nirvana

As you begin to arrive with each step, you become more solid. As you become more solid, you become more free. Solidity and freedom are two aspects of *nirvana*, the state of liberation from craving, fear, and anxiety.

The practice should be pleasant. When you feel happy, your solidity and your freedom will grow, and you will know you are on the path of right practice. You don't need a teacher to tell you if you are enjoying the practice. If you enjoy it, you will feel solid and free. Then you can practice "Solid/Free," as you walk.

Ground of Being

There are two dimensions to life: the historical dimension, in which you identify with birth and death, ups and downs, beginnings and endings; and the ultimate dimension, where you see clearly that all of these are only concepts. As your solidity and freedom grow stronger, you begin to touch the ground of your being, which is the ultimate dimension of reality, and the door of no birth and no death opens.

Touching the Ultimate Dimension

The image often used for the two dimensions of life is that of water and waves. On the ocean's surface, there are many waves—some high, some low, some beautiful, and some less beautiful. All of them have a beginning and an end. But when you touch the waves deeply, you realize that waves are made only of water, and, from the point of view of the water, there is no beginning, no end, no up, no down, no birth, and no death.

When you touch the water—the ground of being—deeply, you can practice the last line of the verse: "In the ultimate, I dwell." As you breathe in, say "Ultimate" with each step, and as you breathe out, say "I dwell." These are not just words. If you really practice them, you will touch the world of no birth and no death with every step.

The Pursuit of Happiness

A llow yourself to *be*. When you practice walking meditation, every step helps you arrive deeply in the present moment. You don't need anything else to touch real happiness.

When your nose is stuffed, it may be difficult to enjoy your breathing. But now you can breathe freely, so please enjoy each breath. That is already peace and happiness. As you breathe out, smile. Exhaling helps expel many toxins. Breathing in and out, especially when the air is not too polluted, is the practice of peace and happiness.

As we cultivate peace and happiness in ourselves, we also nourish peace and happiness in those we love. In fact, we can enjoy each breath and each step for everyone in the ten directions.

Walking with a Child

When you walk, you might like to take the hand of a child. She will receive your concentration and stability, and you will receive her freshness and innocence. From time to time, she may want to run ahead and then wait for you to catch up. A child is a bell of mindfulness, reminding us how wonderful life is.

At Plum Village, I teach the young people a simple verse to practice while walking: *"Oui, oui, oui,"* as they breathe in, and, *"Merci, merci, merci,"* as they breathe out. "Yes, yes, yes. Thanks, thanks, thanks." I want them to respond to life, to society, and to the Earth in a positive way. They enjoy it very much.

Happiness Is Not an Individual Matter

All our ancestors and all future generations are present in us. Liberation is not an individual matter. As long as the ancestors in us are still suffering, we cannot be happy, and we will transmit that suffering to our children and their children.

Now is the time to liberate our ancestors and future generations. It means to free ourselves. If we can take one step freely and happily, touching the Earth mindfully, we can take one hundred. We do it for ourselves and for all previous and future generations. We all arrive at the same time and find peace and happiness together!

Practicing When Angry

When anger arises, walking meditation can be very
helpful. Try reciting this verse as you walk:

Breathing in, I know that anger is in me.
Breathing out, I know this feeling is unpleasant.
[And then, after a while]: *Breathing in, I feel calm.*
Breathing out, I am now strong enough to take care of this anger.

Until you are calm enough to look directly at the anger, just
enjoy your breathing, your walking, and the beauties of the
outdoors. After a while, the anger will subside and you will feel
strong enough to look directly at it, to try to understand its
causes, and to begin the work of transforming it.

Nourishing Steps

Walking meditation is like eating. With each step, we nourish our body and our spirit. When we walk with anxiety and sorrow, it is a kind of junk food. The food of walking meditation should be of a higher quality. Just walk slowly and enjoy a banquet of peace.

Walk for All Beings

The air is cleanest in the early morning and late evening. That is the best time to enjoy walking meditation. Allow the energy of that pure air to enter you.

When you practice walking meditation in the morning, your movements will become smooth and your mind will become alert. You will be more aware of what you are doing all day long. In making decisions, you will find that you are more calm and clear, with more insight and compassion. With each peaceful step you take, all beings, near and far, will benefit.

It's in the Way You Walk

The Buddha printed peace, joy, and serenity on the Earth with each step he took. Thirty years ago, when I visited Gridhrakuta Mountain where the Buddha taught, I walked on the same paths he did. I stood on the Earth where he stood. I sat on the same boulder he sat on. Watching the brilliant red sunset, I knew the Buddha and I were watching the same sun at the same time.

When we walk as the Buddha did, we continue his work. We nurture the seeds of Buddhahood in ourselves and show our gratitude to the Buddha, not by what we say, but by the way we take peaceful, happy steps on the Earth.

I Walk for You

The war in Vietnam caused countless injuries to the minds and bodies of people on both sides. Many soldiers and civilians lost an arm or a leg, and now they cannot join their palms together to pay respects to the Buddha or practice walking meditation. Last year two such people came to our retreat center, and we had to find alternate ways for them to practice walking meditation. I asked each of them to sit in a chair, choose someone who was practicing walking meditation, and become one with him, following his steps in mindfulness. In this way, they made peaceful and serene steps together with their partners, even though they themselves could not walk. I saw tears of joy in their eyes.

Gratefulness

We who have two legs can easily practice walking meditation. We must not forget to be grateful. We walk for ourselves, and we walk for those who cannot walk. We walk for all living beings—past, present, and future.

Walking in Difficult Moments

In 1976, I went to the Gulf of Siam to help the boat people who were adrift at sea. We hired three ships to rescue them and take them to a safe port. Seven hundred people were on our ships adrift at sea when the Singapore authorities ordered me to leave the country and abandon all of them. It was two o'clock in the morning and I had to leave within twenty-four hours.

I knew that if I could not find peace in that difficult moment, I would never find peace. So I practiced walking meditation all night long in my small room. At six o'clock, as the sun rose, a solution came to me! If you panic, you will not know what to do. But practicing breathing, smiling, and walking, a solution may present itself.

Living Deeply

The First Noble Truth taught by the Buddha is the presence of suffering. Awareness of suffering generates compassion, and compassion generates the will to practice the Way.

When I returned to France after trying to help the boat people, life here seemed so strange. I had just seen refugees being robbed, raped, and killed at sea, while in Paris, the shops were filled with every kind of product and people were drinking coffee and wine under neon lights. It was like a dream. How could there be such discrepancies? Aware of the depth of suffering in the world, I vowed not to live superficially.

Walk like a Tiger

When you begin to practice walking meditation, you might feel unbalanced, like a baby learning to walk. Follow your breathing, dwell mindfully on your steps, and soon you will find your balance. Visualize a tiger walking slowly, and you will find that your steps become as majestic as his.

Formless Practice

You don't need to join your palms together or wear a solemn face to practice walking meditation. If possible, choose a quiet path in a park, near a lake, or along a riverbank.

The best practice is formless. Don't walk so slowly that people think you are strange. Walk in a way that others do not even notice that you are practicing. If you meet someone along the way, just smile and continue your walking.

We Need Time

You can practice walking meditation between meetings, on the way to your car, up or down the stairs. When you walk anywhere, allow enough time to practice. Instead of three minutes, give yourself eight or ten. I always leave for the airport an extra hour early, so I can practice walking meditation there. Friends want to keep me until the last minute, but I resist. I tell them that I need the time.

The Path of Awakening

The practice of walking meditation opens your eyes to the wonders and the suffering of the universe. If you are not aware of what is going on around you, where do you expect to encounter ultimate reality?

Every path can be a walking meditation path, from tree-lined roadsides and fragrant rice paddies to the back alleys of Mostar and the mine-filled dirt roads of Cambodia. When you are awake, you will not hesitate to enter any path.

You will suffer, not just from your own worries and fears, but because of your love for all beings. When you open yourself in this way, your companions will be other beings on the path of awakening who share your insight. They will work with you, side by side, to alleviate the world's suffering.

The Seal of an Emperor

Walk upright, with calm, dignity, and joy, as though you were an emperor. Place your foot on the Earth the way an emperor places his seal on a royal decree. A decree can bring happiness or misery. Your steps can do the same. If your steps are peaceful, the world will have peace. If you can make one peaceful step, then peace is possible.

A Flower Blooms beneath Each Step

When the baby Buddha was born, he took seven steps, and a lotus flower appeared under each step. When you practice walking meditation, you can do the same. Visualize a lotus, a tulip or a gardenia blooming under each step the moment your foot touches the ground. If you practice beautifully like this, your friends will see fields of flowers everywhere you walk.

Return to Earth

Imagine that you and I are astronauts. We have landed on the moon, and we find that we cannot return to Earth because our ship's engine is broken beyond repair. We will run out of oxygen before Mission Control in Houston can send another ship to rescue us. We only have two days to live. What would we pray for? What would make us happier than to return to our beautiful planet and walk on it? When confronted with death, we realize the preciousness of walking on the green Earth.

Now we have somehow miraculously survived and have been transported back to Earth. Let us celebrate our joy by walking on our beautiful planet together, with deep peace and concentration.

The Miracle Is to Walk on Earth

People say that walking on water is a miracle, but to me, walking peacefully on the Earth is the real miracle. The Earth is a miracle. Each step is a miracle. Taking steps on our beautiful planet can bring real happiness.

As you walk, be fully aware of your foot, the ground, and the connection between them, which is your conscious breathing. Practice "The Seal of an Emperor," "A Flower Blooms beneath Each Step," or "Return to Earth" as themes for your walking.

This Wondrous World

The Pure Land of Amitabha Buddha is said to have lotus ponds, seven-gem trees, roads paved with gold, and celestial birds. But to me, dirt paths with meadows and lemon trees are much more beautiful. As a novice monk, I told my master, "If the Pure Land does not have lemon trees, I don't want to go there." He may have thought I was stubborn. He didn't say anything.

Later I learned that this world and the Pure Land both come from the mind. That made me very happy. I knew that when you walk mindfully, you are already in the Pure Land.

Walking in the Pure Land

If I had supernatural powers, I would take you to the Pure Land of Amitabha Buddha, where everything is beautiful. But if you bring your worries and anxieties there, you will defile it. To be ready to enter the Pure Land, you have to learn to make peaceful, anxiety-free steps. In fact, if you can learn to take peaceful, anxiety-free steps on the Earth, you won't need to go to the Pure Land. When you are peaceful and free, the Earth itself becomes a Pure Land, and there is no need to go anywhere else.

With Each Step, a Breeze Will Rise

At the entrance of the walking meditation path of a Zen temple in Vietnam, a large stone is carved with these words: "With each step, a breeze will rise." The breeze is the peace and joy that blow away the heat of sorrow. When you walk this way, you do it for yourself and for all beings.

Empty Footprints

Foot and Earth touch.
Bright sunflowers fill our eyes.
In the distance, thunder roars.
Sweat trickles down our cheeks.
Fully entering the world of birth and death,
our tears nourish all beings.
Transcending the world of birth and death,
empty footprints going nowhere.

Through the Deserted Gate

Through the deserted gate,
full of ripened leaves,
I follow the small path.
Earth is as red as a child's lips.
Suddenly
I am aware
of each step
I make.

Take My Hand

Take my hand.
We will walk.
We will only walk.
We will enjoy our walk
without thinking of arriving anywhere.
Walk peacefully.
Walk happily.
Our walk is a peace walk.
Our walk is a happiness walk.

Kiss the Earth

Walk and touch peace every moment.
Walk and touch happiness every moment.
Each step brings a fresh breeze.
Each step makes a flower bloom.
Kiss the Earth with your feet.
Bring the Earth your love and happiness.
The Earth will be safe
when we feel safe in ourselves.

The Earth Is Waiting for You

The Earth is always patient and open-hearted.
She is waiting for you.
She has been waiting for you
for the last trillion lifetimes.
She can wait for any length of time.
She knows you will come back to her one day.
Fresh and green, she will welcome you
exactly like the first time,
because love never says, "This is the last time";
because Earth is a loving mother.
She will never stop waiting for you.

The Welcoming Path

The empty path welcomes you,
fragrant with grass and little flowers,
the path paved with paddy fields
still bearing the marks of your childhood
and the fragrance of mother's hand.
Walk leisurely, peacefully.
Your feet touch the Earth deeply.
Don't let your thoughts carry you away,
Come back to the path every moment.
The path is your dear friend.
She will transmit to you
her solidity,
and her peace.

Come Back

With your mindful breathing,
practice touching the Earth deeply.
Walk as if you are kissing the Earth with your feet,
as if you are massaging the Earth with each step.
Your footprints
will be the marks of an emperor's seal
calling for Now to come back to Here,
so that life will be present,
so that your blood will bring the color of love to your face,
so that the wonders of life will appear,
and all anxieties will be transformed into
peace and joy.

Welcome Back

There were times you did not succeed.
Walking on the empty path, you were floating in the air,
lost in the cycle of birth and death
and drawn into the world of illusion.
But the beautiful path is patient,
always waiting for you to come back,
that path that is so familiar to you,
and so faithful.
It knows you will come back one day.
And it will welcome you back.
The path will be as fresh and as beautiful as the first time.
Love never says that this is the last time.

The Path Is You

That path is you.
That is why it will never tire of waiting.
Whether it is covered with red dust,
autumn leaves,
or icy snow,
come back to the path.
You will be like the tree of life.
Your leaves, trunk, branches,
and the blossoms of your soul
will be fresh and beautiful,
once you enter the practice of Earth Touching.

Walking Peace

Peace is the walk.
Happiness is the walk.
Walk for yourself
and you walk for everyone.

Peace Is Every Step

Peace is every step.
The shining red sun is my heart.
Each flower smiles with me.
How green, how fresh all that grows.
How cool the wind blows.
Peace is every step.
It turns the endless path to joy.

Traditional

I Have Arrived

Thich Nhat Hanh
arrangement: Betsy Rose

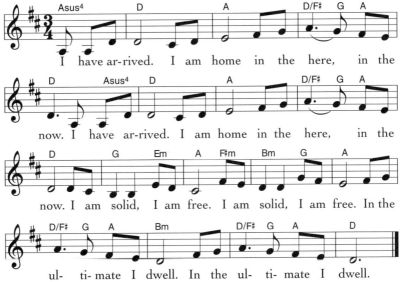

I have ar-rived. I am home in the here, in the

now. I have ar-rived. I am home in the here, in the

now. I am solid, I am free. I am solid, I am free. In the

ul- ti- mate I dwell. In the ul- ti- mate I dwell.

About the Author

Thich Nhat Hanh is a poet, Zen master, and peace activist. The author of seventy-five books, including *Living Buddha, Living Christ*, *Being Peace*, and *Peace Is Every Step*, he was nominated by Martin Luther King, Jr. for the Nobel Peace Prize. In exile from his native Vietnam since 1966, he lives in Plum Village, the meditation community he founded in southwestern France. There he writes, teaches, gardens, and practices mindful walking.

Other Books by Thich Nhat Hanh

Being Peace

The Blooming of a Lotus

Breathe! You Are Alive

Call Me by My True Names

Cultivating the Mind of Love

The Diamond
That Cuts through Illusion

For a Future to Be Possible

The Heart of Understanding

Hermitage Among the Clouds

Interbeing

A Joyful Path

Living Buddha, Living Christ

Love in Action

The Miracle of Mindfulness

Old Path White Clouds

Our Appointment with Life

Peace Is Every Step

Plum Village Chanting and Recitation Book

Present Moment Wonderful Moment

A Rose for Your Pocket

The Stone Boy

The Sun My Heart

Sutra on the Eight Realizations of the Great
Beings

A Taste of Earth

Thundering Silence

Touching Peace

Transformation and Healing

Zen Keys